Arise
A 21-Day Devotional

ARISE

Copyright © 2017 by LaToya Moulton.
All rights reserved.

Produced by:
NyreePress Literary Group
Fort Worth, TX 76161
1-800-972-3864
www.nyreepress.com

All rights reserved. No part of this book may be used or reproduced by any means, graphic, electronic, or mechanical, including photocopying, recording, taping or by any information storage retrieval system without the written permission of the publisher. Copying this book is both illegal and unethical.

ISBN print: 978-1-945304-50-7

Library of Congress Control Number: pending
Categories: Fiction /Christian Living
Printed in the United States of America

LaToya received her certification as a Professional Christian Coach from the Professional Christian Coaching Institute. Her goal for you is to embrace your God-given Potential, tap into your inherent strengths, and confront the limiting beliefs holding you back from being the very BEST Version of YOUR Unique Self!

LaToya is a firm believer in the power of the spoken word and how it has the ability to change and transform anyone's life! Words have the power to build up as well as tare down. LaToya pulls from her very on life lessons of struggle and growth. To discover the BEAUTY of God's Grace and Love!

"God graciously lavished His LOVE upon me! Healing me from the Inside - Out. This transformed my life therefore I am determined to let the LIGHT of Christ SHINE through me. The mission I'm on is to Uplift, Encourage, Inspire and Provoke Women to Arise and set the pace of their day before they start. To become more mindful of the Thoughts and Words they speak!" LaToya

And what better way to become more mindful than to create this amazing tool. A 21 Day Devotional constructed with life speaking affirmations. That were strategically designed to EMPOWER YOU and help JUMP START your morning the right way!

So Let's Arise

xo-LaToya

Dedication

To my love Texan Moulton THANK YOU for pushing me.
We're doing this thing called LIFE together.
Love You.

What are affirmations and how to creatively personalize and implement them into your everyday life!

Webster defines the word Affirmation as: the act of affirming something; a positive assertion; Declaration, Proclamation, Pronouncement, Declare, Proclaim.

Declare: to make known or state clearly, especial in explicit or formals terms, to announce, to manifest; reveal; show.

Declaration: a positive, explicit, or formal statement.

Proclaim: to announce or declare in an open ostentatious way.

LIFT YOUR VOICE and SAY IT LOUD. There is POWER IN YOUR MOUTH! When we affirm something we're not only just simply grouping a set of words together to form a sentence. But we are standing boldly with assertiveness stating something as FACT! That is one of the powerful life speaking aspect affirmations possess. Because it awakens our imagination, the creativeness of our words and the spiritual mountain moving power of our faith! Many people see affirmations as some sort of positive statement that you write out on a note card and put it in your back pocket so your able to rehearse the statement several times throughout the day. O, but there is so much more to it than that! From my own personal journey, I have come to understand that affirmations can help you do, what I like to call, a "mindset check" by reviewing the thoughts you think and the words you speak. Making sure that it all aligns with the common purpose of what your affirming. I considered my affirmations to be a internal accountability system. It helped me keep my inner dialogue and external chatter in check! Keeping the awareness that I stayed align with the common purpose of what I was declaring and affirming in my life.

Do affirmations work? Ok, now I need you to lean in very closely and pay close attention to what I am about to say. Creating personal affirmation is an amazing creative and fun tool to utilize and could be used in a variety of different areas ranging from personal growth/inner transformation, an ultimate goal you have set for yourself, or even a desired mental state of being, it's a good tool for a confidence booster and a great way to repair and build up your self-esteem. However like any good thing it takes TIME, WORK and CONSISTENCY! But if your willing to create and add affirmations to your daily routine of life. I guarantee, you will not be disappointed! It's Powerful! So to answer the question, Of course they do! But it's ALL up to YOU! Your determination and desire to work at it every day, be willing to embrace CHANGE, STRETCH YOURSELF, and STEP OUT of your comfort zone is where you will really begin to see things happen in your life and gain major results! A positive life-speaking affirmation has acceleration power behind it. Therefore, it is mandatory to put ACTION with your FAITH; don't just sit on the side line waiting for the manifestation of a thing—but constantly stay in the place of forward movement, preparation, and implication so that when opportunity presents itself, YOU WILL BE READY to walk through that door. Your words have Creative Power, for example Proverbs 18:21 "Life and Death is in the Power of the tongue." The Power is in Your Mouth! Don't you know that we were created in the image and likeness of a Creative God, who happens to be our Heavenly Father?! He literally created this amazing universe, the earth that we occupy, the birds that fly in the sky, the fish that swim in the sea, every kind of mammal, reptile, and insects that be—even the fruit that grows on the trees. He (God) created it all by a spoken word (Genesis 1:1-2:3) Leading by example, He showed us it could be done. The power of creativity, the power of the spoken word!

When it comes to speaking the promises of God, or life speaking affirmations over your life, it is imperative that your mind aligns! Proverbs 23:7 "For as he thinks within himself, so he is." What you think about is what really matters. How you see yourself is what is most important. For instance, it would be counter-productive for you to confess out of your mouth that you're more than a conquer, when your internal dialogue (thought life) is toxic and says different. This will create a cycle of dysfunction and all but an internal tug-o-war inside of you. Your mouth and mind have to align in order to achieve forward momentum and progress. I'm not saying each day will be as easy as skipping through the tulips, but be open for stretching, and lean into God's Grace and allow the Holy Spirit to minister to you where need be—especially in areas of negative and toxic thinking and speaking. And this leads me to the most vital points of creating and living out effective affirmations. Belief, Meditation, and Repitition—Webster defines the following as...

Meditation: the action or practice of meditating, contemplation, thought, thinking, pondering, reflection, concentration.

Repetition: the action of repeating something that has been said or written; a thing repeated.

Belief: an acceptance of a statement as true; trust, faith, or confidence in something.

The first vital key point, Belief, is a very powerful tool and has the capability to catapult you to new levels, or it can hinder you from truly living your life to its fullest potential. All on account of WHAT YOU BELIEVE to be TRUE about YOU! This vital key point is like a two-sided coin—Positive Beliefs and Negative Beliefs. A Positive Belief within yourself and your God-given capability can empower you to do great exploits. Your words become saturated with His Presence because number one (YOU) decided to come into agreement with what God has to say about You and Your Capabilities! Therefore, there will be an automatic response of your words being affirmative, life-giving, fruitful, edifying, encouraging and up building. For example:

What You Believe You Feed!

A person FULL of Belief, Hope and Positivity YOUR LANGAUGE is DIFFERENT

I am fully capable of doing anything I put my mind to!

I am Full of CAN DO power. Christ resides inside of me, I can do anything!

My past does not define me. My present will not confine me.

ALL things are working together for my good! I move forward with great ambition because my best days are up ahead!

I am grateful for my life! Truly it is a gift. I am blessed beyond measure.

Supernatural favor and abundance overflows into every area of my life. I find ways to be a blessing to others, and I allow my light to shine and glorify My Father which is in Heaven!

I am His Beloved!

Speak words that will empower you!

Positive Belief will get you moving toward dreams even when you do not have all the resources. This type of belief will keep you focused when things become challenging. When you operate from this place, and believe you can do anything, it will cause you to pick yourself up from a defeat or disappointment. Because you believe that you can. You allow yourself to be stretched in ways you didn't know possible. In this realm is where you can begin to see the impossible made possible simply because you believe.

What You Believe You Feed!

A person FULL of Unbelief, Doubt and Negativity YOUR LANGAUGE is DIFFERENT

Do the following look familiar:

"I can't go back to school, I'm too old."

"I can't start a business, I don't have enough money."

"I will never lose the weight."

"I will never get out of this financial rut."

When we allow ourselves to operate from this place of negativity, we begin placing LIMITS on how far we can go and what we're capable of doing. Not much traction will be accomplished here. With this particular mindset, unfortunately, you will find yourself in a cycle of defeat and frustration. Simply because you're limiting Yourself and placing a CAP on your God-given capabilities. Romans 12:2 "Do not conform to this world, but be transformed by the renewing of your mind." The 'renewing of your mind' is a process, and it comes with being committed to daily growth and inner transformation! Taking the truth of God's word and allowing it to saturate your mind, allowing it to be branded upon the tablets of your heart! Come into and FULLY embrace the TRUTH of what God's word has to say about YOU! And begin the daily process of discarding ALL things that DO NOT align/or words that disempower.

Our second vital key point is Meditation. It is imperative that you take time to meditate, ponder, reflect, and think upon your affirmations; let them become a part of you! Now, when you start creating your very own, don't just say it on Monday and allow months to go by before you pick them back up again. Consistency is key!

Which leads us to Repetition as the last vital key point. BE COMITTED. You have to do it every day several times a day. Let your WORDS EMPOWER YOU. Let your WORDS INSPIRE YOU. Speak LIFE to YOURSELF! Listen to me clearly, I AM NOT ENOCURAGING YOU to simply sit around and repeat a vain, lifeless repetition of words. So here is the catch, YOUR BELIEF and CONVICTION in what you're speaking is the GLUE that holds it all together!

What YOU Believe YOU FEED!

Truth to the table, I struggled for years with past experiences of childhood trauma and sexual abuse, low self-esteem, depression, anxiety, and fear. Back then, nothing good came out of my mouth—especially when I was talking about myself—and a lot of it was due to the fact that my vision was broken and blurry, I was unable to SEE beyond my past hurt. So, I operated from that place every day. However, within myself I longed to be FREE. In fact, this devotional was ONE of the things that would not let me rest in that desolate place of brokenness and pain. My Divine Intervention came about in February 2010. Married almost 2 years, I was still carrying internal baggage; masking the hurt. Functioning well so I thought in my dysfunction. I wasn't living the life Christ died to give me. I was holding back and robbing myself of abundance in sweet surrender! Well, on that day, driving in my car, I heard this Still, Small Voice speak so loudly yet only I could hear Him. At the same time, His words were saturated drenched with Love and Grace. The Voice said...

"You can walk around this mountain of defeat for the rest of your life, and you will lose everything. Or, you can choose life and live..."

Driving my car, tears streaming down my face, I knew it was time. I had to GET UP! And MOVE ON from THERE. I will be honest, it wasn't easy. I was used to the dysfunction; it was all I had ever known. Yet, it was time. Therefore, I MADE THE CHOICE...I WANTED TO LIVE! And there began my journey of healing and restoration. On top of diving into the Word of God—and beginning to confess His Truth over my life—it was also imperative that I begin deal with my inner dialogue and unhealthy thought life. I made a personal commitment to daily growth. Aligning my words and thoughts with His. That was MY DAILY choice to speak and think accordingly, REGARDLESS of how I felt within or what I saw with my natural eye on the external. I also sought out professional help and began reading books that spoke to my place of struggle and healing; this aided in my recovery. During this process, I began creating Life-Speaking Affirmations. It helped me tremendously on my journey! It SAVED my life! I believe this is one of the many reason why I am so passionate about Positive Speaking and Personal Affirmations, because I am a living example of what a determined mind and life-speaking, positive words CAN DO!

Many women today are struggling with past experiences of hurt, rejection, childhood trauma, pain, physical and verbal abuse, failure, and disappointment. Due to those life events, they have in turn fostered and nurtured a negative mindset—a nagging, negative narrative that's on repeat in the back of their minds. Which causes many to have a broken and distorted Vision-a broken Vision of themselves; all they SEE is pain and defeat. With a broken Vision of their future, all they SEE is the impossibility of how and why they will not be able to achieve or accomplish a thing. Unable to see clearly, they remain stuck. Pain is Pain. It has no respected person. Race does not matter; gender, religion, financial status, and marital status do not matter. But, you getting up from that place of brokenness and moving on to Living Out and Celebrating Your Amazing Life,that is what matters!

If this is you... if you are struggling in some kind of way, in some area of your life—maybe in pain, or your vision is distorted and broken—allow me to say this, from one SURVIVOR to another: I get it. I've been there. I am GROWING from there right now, with GRACE. The journey never stops. We just go from Glory to Glory! Listen, it is possible to move on into a place of HEALING and RESTORATION. God longs to heal you and desires to be good to you. Today, will you TRUST Him with your pain. Trust Him with the outcome concerning that matter. Believe, and know that He is Good, He desires to be Good to You, and HE WILL CAUSE ALL THINGS to WORK OUT for YOUR GOOD!

When I began creating my very own personal affirmations, the vision that was locked up on the inside of me began to COME A LIVE. Affirmations helped me to define my goals, gain clarity, and also awakened the deepest desires within me that I didn't even know—they had been lying dormant for so many years. Those deep, soul-longing desires were expressed through creative words of hope and inspiration that began to call fourth the God-Size dreams within me—all that God placed within me, before the foundations of the world—from writing, to speaking, empowering women along their journey, and creating tools that would equip and inspire others.

ARISE!

Each morning that you Arise Daughter of God my prayer is that you will NEVER forget Who You are and Who's You are. As you command your day by confessing the truth of God's Word over your life and creating life speaking affirmations that will catapult you into new levels. May your roots forever run deep in His truth! As you awake to NEW mercies every morning may you also embrace the endless possibilities that each day brings to you. May you move forward into each day with power and authority knowing that you are greatly loved, uniquely created, handpicked and O how our Sovereign God knows you by name and He is fully aware of every single detail that concerns your life!

Arise and meet this day!

Arise and embrace your life!

Arise and celebrate as you run your race with grace!

21 DAY DEVOTIONAL

Arise: *appear, emerge, surface, spring up; get or stand up*

Day 1

As I arise to meet this day, I know for a fact that my living is not in vain. I am supposed to be here and that my life does have a purpose. I trust the process and embrace my season as I grow. I declare that I am Blessed and Highly Favored. I am the Head and not the tail. I am the Lender and not the borrower. I am fully equipped to take on this day.
Deuteronomy 28:13

So I Arise!

"The LORD will make you the head, not the tail."

Deuteronomy 28:13

Journal here...

Day 2

As I arise to meet this day, I celebrate the gift of life and offer up a sacrifice of praise. I am thankful for all that God has done, all he is doing and thankful for what He shall do for me in the future. Today my heart is open and overflows with expectancy. For I declare the plans of the Lord is to prosper me and not to harm me. A table of vast abundance is spread before me and I have all I need.
Hebrews 13:15; Jeremiah 29:11; Psalm 23:5-6

So I Arise!

"For I know the plans I have for you," declares the LORD, "plans to prosper you and not to harm you, plans to give you hope and a future.

Jeremiah 29:11

Today I shall...

Day 3

As I arise to meet this day, I embrace the new mercies of my Loving Heavenly Father. I declare today is a New Day which introduces unto me New Opportunities to pursue my dreams and to live my life with passion & enthusiasm. Every individual I come in contact with I will find ways to be a blessing to them. Wither it be through a warm smile or even a word of encouragement.
Lamentations 3:22-23

So I Arise!

Because of the LORD's great love we are not consumed, for his compassions never fail. They are new every morning; great is your faithfulness.

Lamentations 3:22-23

Today I shall arise...

Day 4

As I arise to meet this day, I firmly speak and declare I am NOT a victim but an overcomer. The challenges of life will not break me but makes me stronger and wiser. Daily I am growing, maturing, evolving and learning from all life lessons God allows to come my way. I am Victorious!
Romans 8:37

So I Arise!

No, despite all these things, overwhelming victory is ours through Christ, who loved us.

Romans 8:37

Journal here...

Day 5

As I arise to meet this day, I square my shoulders back, my head held high! And I boldly declare that NEW opportunities are coming my way. Door's of favor are opening up just for me. My Blessings shall not be stopped. Daily the Lord loadeth me with benefits.
Psalm 68:19

So I Arise!

Blessed be the Lord, who daily loadeth us with benefits, even the God of our salvation.
Psalm 68:19

Today I shall...

Day 6

As I arise to meet this day, I immediately open my mouth and offer up Thanksgiving. I am thankful for where God has brought me from. I am thankful for all that I have. I am thankful for this amazing gift called life. And that I have a chance to LIVE IT, therefore, I am determined to give it my best.
Psalm 116:17

So I Arise!

I will offer you a sacrifice of thanksgiving and call on the name of the LORD

Psalm 116:17

Journal here...

Day 7

As I arise to meet this day, I will allow nothing to disturb me. I give love freely and love comes back to me. For I am rooted in the love God. I am placed securely in the palm of His hand and NOTHING shall pluck me out. God is with me. God is for me. God is on my side.
Who can be against me?
John 10:28; Romans 8:38-39

So I Arise!

No power in the sky above or in the earth below-indeed, nothing in all creation will ever be able to separate us from the love of God that is revealed in Christ Jesus our Lord.

Romans 8:39

Today I shall ...

Day 8

As I arise to meet this day, I confess that I love myself. That I am enough and worthy to be loved. I denounce all negative thoughts and only meditate upon those things which are lovely, pure, holy, and of a good report I meditate, ponder and think on these things.
Philippians 4:8-9

So I Arise!

Your thoughts and words have creative power!

Today I shall arise...

Day 9

As I arise to meet this day, I shack off yesterday's cares and I unlatch myself from tomorrow's concerns. I firmly stand and declare that I am present in this very moment. I embrace my NOW with my full undivided attention. My heart is open and ready to receive every Blessing and Lesson that God has in store in for me.
Psalm 37:23

So I Arise!

The LORD makes firm the steps of the one who delights in him; though he may stumble, he will not fall, for the LORD upholds him with his hand.

Psalm 37:23-24

Today I shall...

Day 10

As I arise to meet this day, I confess that my mind is brilliant! Creativity flows through me and from me. I put my hands to work toward my goals and vision. Therefore God blesses it and so it shall prosper. My feet move forward with grace and momentum. I am focused and ready to seize this day.
Proverbs 10:4; Proverbs 21:25

So I Arise!

Failed plans should not be interpreted as a failed vision. Visions don't change, they are only refined. Plans rarely stay the same, and are scrapped or adjusted as needed. Be stubborn about the vision, but flexible with your plans.

John C. Maxwell

Journal here...

Day 11

As I arise to meet this day, My heart is filled with Belief and Hope! That my best days are ahead of me. My past has taught me my present is preparing me and I declare with authority that my future is bright.
Romans 8:28

So I Arise!

And we know that God causes everything to work together for the good of those who love God and are called according to his purpose for them.

Romans 8:28

Today I shall arise...

Day 12

As I arise to meet this day, I envision myself overcoming so I praise God in advance for the victory concerning any obstacle that may come my way. I AM a WINNER. I declare it to be so!
2nd Corinthians 5:7

So I Arise!

For we walk by faith, not by sight

2nd Corinthians 5:7

Today I shall ...

Day 13

As I arise to meet this day, I verbally declare that every area of my life is THRIVING! My mind, body, spirit and soul. My family, finances, relationships, education and business. I bloom and flourish with grace. Nothing or no one shall hold me back.
Psalm 1:3

So I Arise!

They are like trees planted along the riverbank, bearing fruit each season. Their leaves never wither, and they prosper in all they do.

Psalm 1:3

Journal here...

Day 14

As I arise to meet this day, with strength and courage, I affirm that doubt, fear, and discouragement is NOT my portion. As I advance forward with momentum I am determined to make the best out of this day.
Psalm 1:3

So I Arise!

The LORD is my strength and shield. I trust him with all my heart. He helps me, and my heart is filled with joy. I burst out in songs of thanksgiving.

Psalm 28:7

Today I shall arise...

Day 15

As I arise to meet this day, I declare I am a woman on the move. Uncoiled and free from my very own self-limiting beliefs, doubts, negativity and from the fear of man's opinion. In my uniqueness, I CELEBRATE who God created me to be. For I am fearfully and wonderfully made.
Psalm 139:14; Proverbs 29:25

So I Arise!

I praise you because I am fearfully and wonderfully made; your works are wonderful, I know that full well.

Psalm 139:14

Today I shall...

Day 16

As I arise to meet this day, I confess that I am fortified with prayer and praise is my weapon of choice. I will not allow anything to disturb my peace nor steal my joy! For God is with me. God is for me. God is on my side.
Psalm 18:2

So I Arise!

The LORD is my rock, my fortress, and my savior; my God is my rock, in whom I find protection. He is my shield, the power that saves me, and my place of safety.

Psalm 18:2

Journal here...

Day 17

As I arise to meet this day, I take comfort in
knowing that God is good. Therefore He will
do good on my behalf! With confidence,
I embrace this day with both hands.
Proverbs 18:10; Isaiah 41:10

So I Arise!

> The name of the LORD is a strong fortress; the godly run to him and are safe.
>
> Proverbs 18:10

Today I shall arise...

Day 18

As I arise to meet this day, I declare that I am a Woman of Positive Influence. I spread Love and Light everywhere I go. Walking in the newness of life with every step I take. I am fully prepared and equipped for this day.
2nd Corinthians 5:17

So I Arise!

He has given me a new song to sing, a hymn of praise to our God. Many will see what he has done and be amazed. They will put their trust in the LORD.

Psalm 40:3

Today I shall...

Day 19

As I arise to meet this day, I have a made up mind that I will not magnify my problems. But I will magnify God! And declare He is greater and bigger than any of my problems. There is nothing too big that He cannot handle! I confess, that He is fully aware of every matter that concerns my life even down to the little-lest detail.
I am His Beloved!
Psalm 46:1-3

So I Arise!

God is our refuge and strength, always ready to help in times of trouble.
Psalm 46:1

Journal here...

Day 20

As I arise to meet this day, I declare that my emotions are in balance and my thoughts are in check. I will only meditate upon those things that are uplifting, life-giving productive and inspiring. I will only speak those things that are life-giving, encouraging and edifying.
Proverbs 23:7; Proverbs 18:21

So I Arise!

"Watch your thoughts; for they become words. Watch your words; for they become actions. Watch your actions; for they become habits. Watch your habits; for they become character. Watch your character for it will become your destiny."

-Frank Outlaw

Today I shall arise...

Day 21

As I arise to meet this day, I declare that I am an Empowered Woman full of Can Do Power! Who is raising up in her God-given greatness! My roots run deep in the Truth of God's word shattering strong holds gracefully while moving forward with momentum. There is no mountain too high that I can't conquer nor valley too low that I can't overcome. Every crooked path set before me has now been made straight. I declare, God is my help! He has placed my feet on solid ground and anoints me to shatter every glass ceiling that has prevented. I progress riding the waves of life that help shape my character. I Win! Healing and wholeness is my portion! Victory is my portion. Greatness is in my DNA therefore whatever I release into the world it is Good and it shall do Great things!
Psalms 121; Philippians 4:13

So I Arise!

I can do all things through Christ who gives me strength.

Philippians 4:13

Today I shall...

The mercies of God are NEW every single morning, and that introduces to you and I an opportunity of FRESH and NEW possibilities in God!

Arise and greet each day with expectation.
Arise and embrace your current now, knowing that you are never alone and that God is on your side.
Arise with a deep seated knowing that your life has meaning and purpose.
Arise and know that whatever challenge you may be confronted with on today, you are fully equipped and very capable.

www.ingramcontent.com/pod-product-compliance
Lightning Source LLC
Chambersburg PA
CBHW071530080526
44588CB00011B/1629